THE SECRETS OF GASPARILLA

A Pirate Festival Adventure

By

Muhammad Edogi

Table of Contents

INTRODUCTION

The Gasparilla Pirate Festival is an annual celebration in Tampa, Florida, held on the third Saturday of January. This family-friendly event features pirates marching through the city streets, a huge pirate parade, a village of pirate ships and vendors, live music, and plenty of food and entertainment. Each year, tens of thousands of people come out to take part in the festivities, which have been held since 1904.

The Pirate Festival began as a way to commemorate the mythical pirate Jose Gaspar (or Gasparilla), who is said to have plundered the Florida coastline for many years. The parade, which is the highlight of the festival, starts with an impressive procession of flotillas, canons, and pirate ships. People dressed up as pirates march through the city streets with swords, flags, and other pirate accessories to add to the atmosphere.

The day also includes live music, food, and souvenir vendors. There are also competitions, such as the best dressed pirate, best pirate ship, and best pirate chant. At the end of the festival, there is a fireworks show over Tampa Bay.

Overall, the Gasparilla Pirate Festival is a great way to bring the city together and to celebrate the legendary pirate Jose Gaspar. It is a unique and exciting event that has been going on since 1904 and will continue to be a highlight of Tampa's culture in the years to come.

Tampa is one of Florida's vacation hotspots, and anyone who is planning a trip to Florida should seriously consider visiting, even though it is a fair ways from the Miami/Ft. Lauderdale area. The activities in the Tampa area are quite varied, ranging from outdoorsy hiking and fishing opportunities to the nightlife, bars, and restaurants of York City (Tampa's nightlife hotspot). You will also find Busch Gardens and the Florida aquarium in the Tampa area, and these attractions draw thousands of tourists each year. With all of these fantastic opportunities for people of all budgets, ages, and tastes, you may wonder why I will highlight something totally different. The answer essentially boils down to this: I'm a sucker for pirates.

The Gasparilla Pirate Festival is an annual event that Tampa hosts every January. The festival is named after famed pirate José Gaspar, who operated out of the Tampa area back in the Golden Age of piracy. The festival begins when Ye Mystic Krewe of Gasparilla sail into town on a 165' pirate ship, making landfall near downtown Tampa and having a huge parade through the middle of town. It's a crazy time, and certainly my favorite annual festival in Florida (I try to make it over to Tampa each January to catch it).

The Gasparilla Pirate Festival is sandwiched by two other Tampa festivals. A week before, there is a family oriented children's parade, as well as a "Piratechnic Extravaganza" of fireworks launched over Tampa. This is a good festival to bring the whole family to, and is far less crowded than the main "invasion" and pirate parade a week later. A week or two after the parade, you will see the more adult-oriented Sant'Yago Knight Parade, which marches from York City and as such, predictably can get a little blue.

All pirates know that the best way to take in a pirate festival is from a comfortable limousine. Mirage Limo services Tampa and the surrounding area, so it is a natural choice for any reveler who seeks the comfort and luxury that only a limousine can provide - so when you head to Tampa next year for the Pirate Festival, keep that in mind or walk the plank (ye scurvy dogs!)

HISTORY

The History of Gasparilla Pirate Festival

Gasparilla Pirate Festival is an annual celebration of Tampa's mythical pirate heritage, located in Tampa Bay, Florida. The event has been held since 1904 and is one of the oldest pirate festivals in the United States. The festival is named after the legendary pirate Jose Gaspar, a Spanish naval officer who became a powerful pirate in the late 18th and early 19th centuries.

The festival began as a small affair with just a few people dressing in pirate costumes and carrying flags while they sailed around the bay. Over the years, it has grown into a large-scale event with hundreds of boats, elaborate parades, and lots of music and entertainment.

Today, the festival is one of the most popular events in the city and is attended by thousands of people each year. It is a celebration of Tampa's maritime history and includes a range of activities such as re-enactments of battles between Jose

Gaspar and the US Navy, a pirate parade, costumed characters, and the crowning of a Pirate King and Queen.

Gasparilla Pirate Festival has become an important part of Tampa's local community. The event brings in a lot of revenue for the city and is a great way for people to get together and celebrate Tampa's rich culture and history. This annual event has become a beloved tradition in Tampa and is sure to live on for years to come.

Gasparilla the pirate was born around 1756 in Seville, Spain. He joined the Spanish navy at an early age and was so successful in his service to Spain that he became an admiral. He was not an easy man to get along with and some would say Gasparilla was an antagonist. This behavior eventually caused so many problems that he had to run away from his service and lead a life of piracy.

Disenfranchised with Spain, Jose Gasparilla, put together a pirate crew hell bent on making their home country pay a price by attacking her ships and stealing their treasure. His main area of piracy was along the coast of Florida. This was where Spain's treasure fleet sailed on their way home. By 1795 his pirate crew was so successful that they captured over 35 of Spain's ships and amassed a huge fortune in pirate treasure. The problem with having so much Spanish silver and gold was where to store it or hide it.

Gasparilla had the answer. He overtook an island of the coast of Boca Grande and renamed it Gasparilla Island. He and his band of pirates worked the waters off of Florida for almost 30 years. So, you can imagine how much treasure or loot they must have amassed in that time.

Jose Gasparilla and his pirates came to an end in 1821 when the United States warship, the Enterprise, attacked him and sent him to Davey Jones Locker with an anchor chain tied around his waist. He and his crew never divulged where the mass of the treasure was buried. It is a fair assumption that it must be somewhere among the islands around Gasparilla Island

Events

The winter is when the most popular festivals and events occur in Tampa. This is mainly due to the sweltering heat and frequent rain that occurs in the summertime. The weather is usually perfect this time of year in the 70s with little to no rain. Sometimes a cold front may come through and spoil the fun making it somewhat "chilly" in the 60s. Of course this is a heat wave to people from the north during this time of year. We are so spoiled in this part of the country.

Gasparilla Pirate Fest

The Gasparilla Pirate Fest is the signature event during the winter for the city of Tampa. The pirate is somewhat of a mascot for Tampa, considering the Tampa Bay Buccaneers. These festival started decades ago dating back to 1904. It is based on the legendary pirate Jose Gaspar who is thought to have ruled the Tampa Bay area in the 1800s.

Hundreds of thousands of people come to the Tampa area from all over the country each year dressed in pirate costumes and sporting beads around their necks.

The day begins with the invasion. This is where a pirate ship floats into downtown Tampa surrounded by hundreds of smaller vessels and boats. The crew comes into the city and stages a mock invasion where they capture the key to the city from the mayor.

After the invasion thousands of people line up along the roads for the parade. As the parade commences individuals scream, wave and try to get the attention of the people on the floats to toss beads their way. Sort of like a mini version of Mardi Gras.

The parade concludes and the partying continues throughout the night with live music, concerts, food and festivities.

Also as part of the Gasparilla celebration there are 2 other parades during the month. The Gasparilla Children's Parade takes place a week before the Pirate fest. This parade caters toward the little ones with air shows, face painting, and entertainment followed by a fireworks display.

The Knight parade takes place usually a couple of weeks after the main Gasparilla festival. This parade occurs at night through downtown and York City and is catered to an adult crowd.

Florida State Fair

Who can resist turkey legs, funnel cake, and whatever you can think have fried? That is why the Florida State Fair is one of the most popular events in the city. Food, rides, and shows basically sums up what the Florida State Fair is all about.

This yearly event takes place every February at the Florida State Fairgrounds. Thousands of people from all over the state attend each year.

At the fair you will find a variety of entertainment. Events such as circus shows, wrestling matches, and animal shows are the norm. All of the typical fair rides will also be found throughout the fairgrounds, including Ferris wheels, air rides, etc.

Florida Strawberry Festival

The Florida Strawberry Festival is another popular event that takes place each year in the Tampa Bay area. This festival is held every year in March in nearby Plant city, a 25 minute drive from Tampa.

The Strawberry Festival is where thousands come every year to get their fix of strawberries and concerts galore, mostly country music. You will find strawberry pies, shortcakes, smoothies and anything else strawberry that you can think of.

Some of the country music artists that have performed in the past include Johnny Cash, Garth Brooks, Jessica Simpson, Loretta Lynn and Taylor Swift.

GASPARILLA INVASION

The Gasparilla Invasion is the main event of the Gasparilla Pirate Festival. On the Saturday before the parade, a replica pirate ship sails into downtown Tampa and is greeted by the mayor and other officials. After the mayor presents the Key to the City to the pirate captain, the pirates disembark and march through the city in a parade.

Tampa Florida is a city located in the Gulf Coast Bay in Florida and is home to an estimate of 350,000. Today, the city is part of the Tampa Bay metropolitan area, and attracts thousands of people each year. If you're planning a vacation for the summer, but don't know where to go yet - you might want to consider visiting Tampa, Florida. Here are the top five reasons as to why Tampa, Florida should be on your vacation list:

Reason 1: Lots of Outdoor Activities

Tampa, Florida was ranked as the 5th for best cities for outdoor enthusiasts. This is because the city has numerous choices when it comes to outdoor activities. There are plenty of botanical gardens, theme parks, beaches and several zoos within the city and the surrounding suburbs that will certainly put a lot of fun and enjoyment in your vacation. Some popular parks include the Hillsborough River State Park, The Adventure Island, The Florida Aquarium, Busch Gardens Tampa Bay and The Lowry Park Zoo, which is home to over 2000 species of animals.

Reason 2: Plenty of Exciting Events

Tampa is also known for several exciting and fun events, especially the Gasparilla, which is held usually in January or February. The Gasparilla Priate festival is a based pirate invasion which has been held ever since 1904. The festival is also popularly known as the "Mardi Gras" of the city, which involves flotillas and parades. The parade draws almost 500,000 attendees from all over the country. Aside from that, Tampa has a lot more going with a number of other festivals including related to the Gasparilla such as the Distance Dance, International Film Festival and the Outback

Bowl. Other non pirate-themed celebrations include the Fiesta Day, the Tampa International Gay and Lesbian Festival, the GaYbor Days and the Sant'Yago Knight Parade, which is an adult oriented parade.

Reason 3: Fun Sports Attractions

The city of Tampa is located in the Tampa Bay Metropolitan area, which is represented in the National Football League by the Tampa Bay Buccaneers; in the National Hockey League by the Tampa Bay Lightening and in Major League Baseball by the Tampa Bay Rays. These teams regularly train in the area or in the nearby cities, and host a variety of games per year.

Reason 4: Numerous Accommodation Choices

Tampa, Florida is visited by hundreds of thousands of tourists each year, so it is natural for the city to have numerous accommodation options to meet your needs, budget and preferences.

GASPARILLA PARADE

The Gasparilla Parade is one of the main events of the Gasparilla Pirate Festival. The parade includes floats, marching bands, and costumed pirates. The parade begins at Bayshore Boulevard and proceeds down Hillsborough Avenue. The parade is attended by thousands of spectators and is televised by loc The Gasparilla Parade is an iconic Tampa tradition that dates back to 1904. It is a celebration of the city's pirate heritage, featuring a flotilla of pirate ships on the Hillsborough river, marching bands, dancers, and the infamous Gasparilla Parade King and Queen.

The parade takes place each year on the last Saturday of January, and has become one of the most anticipated events in Tampa. The parade starts at Bay to Bay Boulevard and Bay shore Boulevard and runs through the downtown area, ending at the Tampa Convention Center.

The parade is attended by thousands of people, with many watching from balconies or the street.

During the parade, attendees can enjoy live music, floats, and colorful costumes. There are also special activities for kids, such as face painting, balloon artists, and carnival-style games.

At the end of the parade, the Gasparilla Pirate King and Queen are presented as they disembark from their ships in the harbor. The parade is also accompanied by a fireworks display, making it a truly spectacular event.

The Gasparilla Parade is a beloved Tampa tradition that brings people together to celebrate the city's history and culture. It's a great opportunity for the whole family to have a fun-filled and unforgettable day.al television stations.

Gasparilla Pirate Fest

The Gasparilla Pirate Fest is the last event of the Gasparilla Pirate Festival. The Pirate Fest includes several days of live entertainment, activities, and food. There are also several pirate-themed events, such as a treasure hunt, costume contests, and a pirate market. The pirate market is a popular attraction for festival-goers, as it features items from local merchants and artisans.

The Gasparilla Pirate Fest is an annual celebration of pirate culture that takes place on the streets of Tampa, Florida. It is one of the most popular festivals in the United States and is known for its colorful floats, pirate-themed costumes, and lively parades.

The festival celebrates the legend of José Gaspar, an 18th century Spanish pirate who is said to have terrorized the Gulf of Mexico. The festival typically consists of a parade that winds through downtown Tampa, and a coronation ceremony where a local celebrity is crowned “Ye Mystic Krewe of

Gasparilla".

The festival is known for its lively parade, which typically includes marching bands, floats, and horseback riders. During the parade, many of the participants dress up in pirate costumes and throw beads and other items to the crowd. After the parade, a large party takes place at the Tampa Convention Center.

The festival also includes activities such as a 5k run, a festival village, and a fireworks display. The festival village typically features food, music, and vendors selling pirate-themed merchandise.

The Gasparilla Pirate Fest is a great way to celebrate the city's rich history and culture. Thousands of people from all over the country flock to Tampa each year to take part in the festivities. Whether you're a fan of history or just looking for a great day of fun, the Gasparilla Pirate Fest is definitely an event not to be missed.

Dozens of festivals and events take place in Tampa Bay every year and all year long. The biggest and most famous one is the Gasparilla Pirate Festival. It is a mock pirate invasion and an enormous celebration with four hundred thousand participants.

It has been a major event since 1904 and is organized between January and February. Other Gasparilla festivities are celebrated until the month of March, such as the Gasparilla Festival of the Arts, the Sant'Yago Knight Parade and the Gasparilla Children's Parade, the Gasparilla Distance Classic and the Gasparilla International Film Festival.

All of these festivals as well as the Clearwater Jazz Festival, where different musicians perform every year, can be enjoyed for free. People bring lawn chairs and watch celebrities like Richie Cole and Dave Brubeck in an open area.

Not every event is free, however, but there are tons of very cheap events going on in Tampa. Last year, fans went crazy when USF football season tickets were sold for super low prices such as $ 6.50. People had their dreams come true watching

Tampa Bay Rays games for cheaper than a hamburger.

Tampa hosts many other events during the year, such as the annual Florida State Fair. This Fair lasts for eleven days and people can participate in competitions and try fun food. The Florida Strawberry Festival is a very traditional festival with a parade and takes place in late spring around the time of the strawberry harvest.

Tampa also offers attractions that can be visited all year long, such as the Lowry Park Zoo, a unique zoo for its interactive exhibits. At the interactive discovery center, visitors can ride camels, pet and feed animals and enjoy activities such as the river eco-tour and encounters with West Indian Manatees. As a nonprofit organization, the Lowry Park Zoo can be visited free.

Tampa has beautiful beaches that are visited by people from all over the world. The North Beach at Fort De Soto Park is the most famous one in the area and in the United States, it is considered to be one of the best beaches in the country. It is always full of residents and tourists enjoying amazing beach breaks.

However, Tampa also has beaches for people who are looking for different ways of enjoying a sunny day. Caladesi Island State Park is an island with beautiful and calm beaches and mangroves that can be visited by kayak. Thus, it is not too frequented and a perfect place to relax.

Siesta Key Beach, which is famous for having the whitest sand in the world, is another gorgeous beach while the Blind Pass Beach with dunes can offer lots of fun. There is a beach for all tastes and ages in Tampa but in any case, one is going to be astonished by their natural beauty.

With all of these entertainment options, there will not be enough time to enjoy all of it and there is no doubt about it that many tourists decide to come back to appreciate all the other attractions that were missed out on.

Conclusion

The Gasparilla Pirate Festival is a unique and exciting event that takes place annually in Tampa, Florida. The festival is a celebration of the legendary pirate Jose Gaspar and his supposed reign of terror on the Gulf of Mexico in the late 1700s and early 1800s.

The festival begins with the "invasion" of the city by the Gasparilla Krewe, a group of pirates who sail into Tampa Bay on a ship called the José Gasparilla. They are met by the mayor of Tampa, who surrenders the city to the pirates in a mock ceremony.

The main event of the festival is the Gasparilla Pirate Parade, which is one of the largest parades in the Southeast. The parade features floats, marching bands, and thousands of participants dressed as pirates, who toss beads and other trinkets to the crowds lining the parade route.

In addition to the parade, the festival also includes a variety of other events, such as a pirate invasion reenactment, a children's parade, and a pirate village with food, drinks, and live music.

Overall, the Gasparilla Pirate Festival is a colorful and lively event that attracts thousands of visitors to Tampa each year. It is a unique celebration of history and tradition that offers something for everyone, from families with young children to adults looking for a fun and exciting time.

In conclusion, the Gasparilla Pirate Festival is a unique and exciting event that offers a wide range of activities and entertainment for all ages. It is a celebration of the legendary pirate Jose Gaspar and his supposed reign of terror on the Gulf of Mexico in the late 1700s and early 1800s. The festival is a must-see for anyone visiting Tampa during the month of January and is a great way to experience the rich culture and history of this vibrant Gulf Coast city.

www.ingramcontent.com/pod-product-compliance
Lightning Source LLC
LaVergne TN
LVHW020544160826
845677LV00015B/4191

* 9 7 9 8 3 7 5 2 2 3 1 5 5 *